EIGHT MADRIGALS

BY ELIZABETHAN COMPOSERS

arranged for

S.S.A. and S.S.A.A.

CONTENTS

ISBN 0-85360-663-3

9 780853 606635

NOVELLO

EXCLUSIVELY DISTRIBUTED BY

HAL•LEONARD®

Order No: NOV 490361

THE NIGHTINGALE

MADRIGAL

COMPOSED BY

THOMAS WEELKES.

(A.D. 1600.)

ARRANGED FOR FEMALE VOICES BY HENRY LESLIE.

London: NOVELLO AND COMPANY, Limited

The black-bird and . . the thrush, . . And all the pret - ty

The black-bird and . . the thrush, And all the pret - ty cho-ris-

black - bird and . . . the thrush, And all the pret - ty cho-ris-ters of

cho - ris-ters of flight, That chaunt their mu - sic notes on ev - 'ry

- ters of flight, That chaunt their mu - sic notes on ev - - 'ry

flight, That chaunt their mu - sic notes on ev - 'ry bush, that

bush, that chaunt their mu - sic notes on ev - 'ry bush. bush. Let

bush, that chaunt their mu - sic notes on ev - - 'ry bush. bush. Let

chaunt . . their mu - sic notes . . on ev - 'ry bush. bush. Let

1st time. *2nd time.*

3

THE NIGHTINGALE.

them no more con-tend who shall ex-cel, The cuc-koo, cuc-koo, the

them no more con-tend who shall ex-cel, ... The cuc-koo, cuc-koo,

them no more con-tend who shall ex-cel, ... The cuc-koo, the cuc-

cuc-koo, cuc-koo, cuc-koo, the cuc-koo, cuc-koo, cuc-

the cuc-koo, cuc-koo, cuc-koo, the cuc-koo, cuc-koo

-koo is the bird, the cuc-koo is the bird, the

-koo, cuc-koo, cuc-koo, cuc-koo is the bird that bears the bell.

is the bird, cuc-koo, cuc-koo, cuc-koo is the bird that bears the bell.

cuc-koo is ... the bird ... that bears .. the bell.

THE NIGHTINGALE.

Seek sweet content.

ADAPTED FOR S.S.A. FROM WILBYE'S MADRIGAL "FLY, LOVE, TO HEAVEN."

London: NOVELLO AND COMPANY, Limited

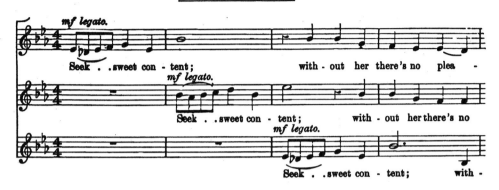

NOW IS THE MONTH OF MAYING

BALLET

BY

THOMAS MORLEY

(1595)

ARRANGED FOR FEMALE VOICES (S.S.A.A.) BY JOHN E. WEST

LONDON: NOVELLO AND COMPANY, LIMITED

COME AGAIN! SWEET LOVE

PART-SONG FOR FOUR VOICES

BY

JOHN DOWLAND

FROM 1st BOOK OF "SONGS AND AYRES IN FOURE PARTS," (No. XVII.)
ARRANGED FOR FEMALE VOICES (S.S.A.A.) BY JOHN E. WEST

LONDON: NOVELLO AND COMPANY, LIMITED

The original four-part version is published in THE MUSICAL TIMES, No. 164

To see, to hear, to touch, to kiss, to die . . . .
I sit, I sigh, I weep, I faint, I die . . . .

To see, to hear, to touch, to kiss, to die, to die With
I sit, I sigh, I weep, I faint, I die, I die In

To see, to hear, to touch, to kiss, to die, ...
I sit, I sigh, I weep, I faint, I die, ...

To see, to hear, to touch, to kiss, to die, to
I sit, I sigh, I weep, I faint, I die, I

(More prominent than the other voices to the end of the verse)

[Repeat optional]

. . . With thee a - gain in sweet-est sym - - pa - thy.
In dead-ly pain, and end-less mis - - er - y.

thee a - gain, a - gain in sweet - est . . sym - - pa - thy.
dead - ly pain, in pain, and end - less . . mis - - er - y.

. . . . to die With thee a - gain in sweet-est sym - - pa - thy.
I die In dead-ly pain, and end-less mis - - er - y.

die With thee a - gain in sweet - est sym - - pa - thy.
die In dead - ly pain, and end - less mis - - er - y.

[Repeat optional]

15

WHAT SAITH MY DAINTY DARLING

BALLET

BY

THOMAS MORLEY

(1595)

ARRANGED FOR FEMALE VOICES (S.S.A.A.) BY JOHN E. WEST

London : NOVELLO AND COMPANY, Limited

Also published for Mixed Voices in THE ORIANA, No. 82.

ALL CREATURES NOW ARE MERRY MINDED

MADRIGAL
BY
JOHN BENNET

(No. 5 of "The Triumphs of Oriana")
*ARRANGED FOR S.S.A.

London: NOVELLO & COMPANY, Limited

*From the original edition for S.S.A.T.B. edited by Lionel Benson in THE ORIANA, No. 5.

flow-'ry gar-lands crown-ed, Queen_ of all queens re-

flow-'ry gar-lands crown-ed, Queen_ of all queens re - nown -

flow-'ry gar-lands crown-ed, Queen_ of all queens, queen_ of all

-nown - ed, Queen of all queens re - nown - ed. Then

-ed, Queen of all queens re - nown - - - - ed. Then

queens, Queen_ of all queens re - nown - - - ed. Then

sang the Shep-herds and Nymphs of Di - a - na, Nymphs of Di - a - na,

sang the Shep-herds and Nymphs of Di - a - na, Nymphs of Di - a - na, "Long

sang the Shep-herds and Nymphs of Di - a - na, Nymphs of Di - a - na,

THE SILVER SWAN

MADRIGAL

BY

ORLANDO GIBBONS

(1612)

ARRANGED FOR FEMALE VOICES (S.S.A.A.) BY JOHN E. WEST

London: NOVELLO AND COMPANY, LIMITED

more. Fare - well all joys, O death, come close mine

more. Fare - well all joys, O.. death,.. come close mine.. eyes, close mine

more. Fare - well all joys, O..... death,.. come ... close mine eyes; More

more. Fare - well all joys, O death, come close mine eyes;

eyes; More geese than swans now live, more fools than wise.

eyes; More geese than swans now live, more fools .. than ... wise.

geese than swans now live, more fools, than wise, than ... wise.

More geese than swans now live, more fools than wise.

MY BONNY LASS SHE SMILETH

MADRIGAL

BY

THOMAS MORLEY

(1595)

ARRANGED FOR FEMALE VOICES (S.S.A.A.) BY JOHN E. WEST

LONDON: NOVELLO AND COMPANY, LIMITED

MY BONNY LASS SHE SMILETH

MY BONNY LASS SHE SMILETH